PASSION

PASSION

poems

Judith H. Montgomery

DEFINED PROVIDENCE
1999
CHAPBOOK CONTEST SELECTION

CHOSEN BY MARK DOTY

Acknowledgments

Grateful acknowledgment is made to the editors of the following journals, in which these poems first appeared:

The Alembic: "This is the time we're going to be dying"
The Bellingham Review: "The White Boat"
The Formalist: "Card Party"
The Nebraska Review: "Cardioversion"
Moveo Angelus Literary Arts: "Penelope's Handmaiden;" "Light, and Other
      Radiation"
Red Rock Review: "Gallop;" "Sting"

"The White Boat" was selected by Charles Wright as winner of the 49th Parallel Poetry Prize.

"Gallop" was selected by Alberto Rios for the Red Rock Poetry Award.

My thanks to Literary Arts, Inc., for an Oregon Literary Arts fellowship that helped support preparation of this book.

Particular thanks also to Nance Van Winckel, Christopher Howell, Bruce Smith, Jane Glazer, and Joseph Millar for invaluable advice on the shape of the chapbook and the poems, and to Suzan Hall for advice on esthetics.

Published by Defined Providence Press
P.O. Box 16143, Rumford, Rhode Island 02916

Typeset in Garamond

Cover art: photograph by Jerry Atkin

ISBN 0-9673495-0-8

FIRST EDITION

For Phillip

Table of Contents

Drought   1
Rose/Wood   3
Sting   6
Aftermath   7
Penelope's Handmaiden   9
Forecast: One Stays, One Goes   10
Light, and Other Radiation   11
Principia Erotica   13
Wake   14
Blue Horse Weather   16
Blue Hook   18
Blue Ice/Blue Fist   19

Wake-Robin   23
Arson   25
Card Party   26
Gallop   27
The White Boat   28
This is the time we're going to be dying   30
Abduction   31
Breast: Still   32
Cardioversion   34
The Photographer's Father   36
Imagining Their Departure   38
Passion   39

DROUGHT

They agreed to lie
apart, heat-split in bed.

Salt mortar hardening
between them on the sheets.

Grateful. They were
grateful for excuse.

No conduit of speech.
No pressing flesh.

All week the heat set,
gluing words to walls. Incinerating sills.

At midnight his cigarette
burned its heart behind the kitchen screen.

Her face cracked in silver ash,
a flickering in attic panes.

Dog moon scorched the tinder sky.
Thunder rattled tin.

Then lightning caught,
and without warning, drought broke.

The mountain shook loose
ropes of roily clouds.

White curtains snapped at glass,
gutters overspilled.

They fled the house,
flinching under rain-chill.

A godsend, the neighbor called
from the fence—*the down pour* . . .

What could they do but nod, rooted
separate and wet on the slumping porch?

ROSE/WOOD

She's decked her room for tongues and trouble.
Smoked silk scarves across the lamps.

Glossed eggshell paint on wall and lintel,
lemon-oiled the rosewood bed

where he and she have August-rubbed
flushed skin on greedy skin,

pennies burnished by abrasion.
They've spent thirty fire-coin moons

hot-locked in click and grin of passion:
tooth and tangle, bodies' range laid

plain: belly of the upper arm, mouth
of thigh, downsoft hidden earlobe slide . . .

*

each coupling drowned in rose-tides—
Sweet Surrender lapping at the sill,

his Sunday saffron-roses' scent
pouring from the cobalt vase, bedside.

He trails blossoms underneath
her chin, breastbloom, belly, knee

and she reflects like buttercups
the gleam of skinshine where he strokes—

nape to knob to buttocks' rise—
lipping petals down her glowing back.

*

Tonight she lights her skin against fall dark.
His ivory roses shimmer in the vase.

She plummets with him under cover. Gauze
cascades, shredded from her thudding bed.

The fragile canopy casts its shadows
down the four polished posts

that shudder in heat of hothouse bloom.
Sheets fall, tinder petals to the floor,

as he and she burst hot against the rose-
wood bed that jitters close to demolition.

Scarves slide to the edge of scorch,
the lampbulb shakes and smokes.

The dresser mirror splintering,
shards waiting for the blind unwary foot . . .

                    *

And then he leans, half-buckled, leaving,
in a gloss of sweat and fresh pale paint,

and scrapes some words—*it's best,
done, over*—from his broken plate.

Over/other/move/love: she seizes
in rose-naked hands the cobalt vase

and hurls it—water, petal, stamen, pistil—
at the doorframe he's abandoned

4

and so shatters crystal, gouges
unmarked eggshell wall and wood.

Broken-spined, his ivory roses lie.
Red oak floorboards soak, bleach.

*

Midnight: beyond the lamps, she hears
Surrender's brittle branches scrape

against the windowglass as though to peel
gone-dry leaves to stem, to woodheart.

Crouching wound in bandages of sheet,
she soothes her wall's wounds

with tender absolutions: sand-
paper fanned up coarse to fine.

She gutters spackle. Skirts a petal
lacquered at the bottom of the can.

Contemplates the wire brush,
draws it down her kissburned cheek:

she cannot scrub away the fire-
crisped leaf, thorn curved deep, red rose hip

still burning. She lifts the brush.
She will repair what she can reach.

STING

The wasp who lives in the ceiling lamp
emerges just as we've forgotten him.
Crawls out cloaked in night-stiff wings.
Bears his black needle, emblem of office,
as though it were a thing of no import.

Screwed in tight above our bed,
his home's a glass bowl etched opaque.
We lie below. We can't make out
his scheme. Tell if he hides alone.
If he burnishes his sting and dreams of us.

At dawn we wake to his black blur.
At midnight think of our ladder
ready on the stair. Imagine *smack*.
We try his will—crank the window
wide. He will not leave. He's ours.

We could push our bed aside. Erect
the ladder. Climb. But once we admit
he's there—would he attack? Unstitch
the bed, the room, the house? We hold
our fire: every bedroom has its sting.

AFTERMATH

It is no good: not the site,
not the thunder of the creek
beating the river's body.
Not the tent, sagging off poles
where it was meant to peak.

They struggle silently with knots
to peg opposing sides. She stirs
the soup. He hunches over luke-
warm beans, deflecting conversation.
She lets him. Then the storm.

They fling plates into a box,
prop the drowning lantern with a rock.
Duck the green flail—leaves stripped
by needle hail. Gasp at a crack
of light, slam into the shaking tent.

There is, for twenty minutes,
a bold excitement: the torn flap
caught with twine, the two bodies
huddled under bang and flare.
Ignition, keyed to old passion.

Reflex electricity. A certain
glare. The double bag unzipped
and zipped again. The four pent
limbs squirming out of jeans,
the coupling lit by lightning. Still,

it is no good. Their eyes gleam,
below and above, feral as cats
lashed and lashing in a cave.
Who could tell who won?
Sullen night. Tight-lipped dawn.

*

Packed, they baby the old pickup
over gravel sumps and berry wands,
hurry to be gone. At sixty feet,
the forest ranger flags them down.
Did you hear it? The last strike?

They leave the motor running.
Behind, a Ponderosa smoldering
to cinnamon is peeled, in a great
slow spiral down the trunk,
bark scored to cambium.

Shards the size of saplings flung
beyond the road, crushing lupine,
fern. The husband lifts the camera.
She watches, from a distance,
his practiced snap. Then turns

away, to the ranger: *Will it live?*
He shakes his head, rubs a stubbled jaw.
It'll live, he says, *but that one side
down the wound*—he turns her
with a touch—*won't branch again.*

At the trunk, she strokes the bark
spared, then the new wound
glowing—as though the tree has been
anaesthetized, and buried nerves
do not know the damage yet.

PENELOPE'S HANDMAIDEN

The sky that day—
the finest comb of fleece
tendered from the lamb's washed flank.

And music—
the pluck of waves unstrung at shore,
the rubbing of ships' shattered planks.

Beyond the walls,
the grapes hung barely by a finger
from bent vines, perfume leaking through their arms.

On the back of my hand
my lady's red slap—
ripe suspicious fear laid out in five fast lines.

Once I dreamed my Lord
returned and stormed the hall,
demanding the burial cloak always on the loom.

Should I have lent my fingers
to reweave her purple work and earned
my Lord's fond glance or sliding touch again?

Tonight, I will hide
my hand within a scraped wool wrap
when I tell the courting lords how to watch her.

Or not. Sometimes, they say,
the gods send warnings, threaded
on a loom, tricked out in foam-flecked sea,

or opened
in the speaking trunks of trees—
but not to the handmaid. There will be

no charitable answers for me.

FORECAST: ONE STAYS, ONE GOES

At dawn, a sparrow—wind-
spat against our bedroom sill.

Spent feather felled on sheets
stripped empty of your heat.

The paperboy splits apart
the pot of red geraniums—

small bloody petals spill
in auguries of weather:

No rain again this week.
A white sun cracks the glaze of sky.

Dry lightning fires at Random Peak.
The moon will spike low tide.

No forecast's made for heart-
lines stalled in a dead calm eye

while all July's barometers
fix as one at blue.

LIGHT, AND OTHER RADIATION

The peak pitches white above the broken lake.
The tent is pegged in place beyond wake's reach.
Their sleeping bags lie falsely flank by flank,

the lantern hung to light them to the beach.
A late swim to the dock through glacial water
seals them, breath and body, against touch.

The physicist and the poet's daughter,
wet-suited, silent, watch the darkening cove
where light slices waves, and ice loiters.

She tries a gambit, hoping to disprove
his distance: asks why a lake is blue, and sky.
He lectures her on leptons and Cherenkov

radiation—light slow-bent from true, a sly
erudition that begs her dreamer's question
and dangles in her face a baser why:

why he has cycled twenty days past home,
nor looked, nor stopped, but to collect his things.
Why she counts echoes in the mute phone—

his promises deflected, the absent ring.
Light slows, he drives inexorably on, *in all
matter but a vacuum. Bends. While spitting*

*by, electrons unimpeded buzz a blue fall,
glow bold in water, scintillate in cut stone.*
Above the lake, Diamond Peak flares, sun stalls

copper on the rocks and whitened bones
picked over by predator and winter.
She shivers. He rises, and the boards groan.

Dives without a word or glance, and leaves her
to make her way alone. She thinks of spoons
in water, light-bent. Of facets turned to factors.

Is forced to mark his angle: the thing that's true
is writ in light and ice: bent is always blue.

PRINCIPIA EROTICA

When all was said
& undone, he reckoned

the puzzle of elements
jumpy in equation:

the not-quite parallel
legs of their compass

the triangles of fur
his cylinder, her diamond

parallelogram
his male torso

sine wave
her woman's

sloping cones
of her breasts

radii wheeling
from his nipples

paired columns
of flushed necks

the fractals blooming
upward from their spines

the bilaterality
his eye her eye, her lip his swollen lip

their story problem—
straight-arrow theory clasping chaos—

exponentials of explosion
intersections of desire.

WAKE

In midnight's cobalt hush I play
us like a movie in my head—

moon-bright beach, white tide
of stars. Paired sandsteps, lips,

the rest. I float my four-poster
on the salt surf of the dream—

body-lit in phosphor rush,
blissed above abyss.

But my film spins off its reel.
Ocean growls coal-black and tin,

drags my bed-board under seas
sharp as moon's blade-edge.

I call your name out as I crouch
beneath a breaker hammering high

but you are safe, jetty-side—
back turned to shoot the sickle-moon.

Blue-skinned, I ride against riptide
that sucks my black-and-white shore bare,

exposing rock and cliff and bone—
the jagged fearful edges of my bed.

Then hurl hard home to meet
the glitter-fracture of the beach.

The film rewinds. Drags me back in.
I've countered with small spells of pharmacy—

grains gleaming in broken shells.
They drown in your white wake—

seadrug that wrecks and ruins me.
I do no dream but you.

BLUE HORSE WEATHER

This poem's not about winter weather
howling down the gorge—or black ice that spares
no blade or bough cracking under blue
crystal—midnight wind that scours cover—
or approving stars that sanction snow
sleeting down the flanks of a lost, chill horse.

It's night, it's bleak night, and the neighbor's horse
is stalled safe in oats and straw, weather-
ing the storm in a sturdy high-beamed barn. Snow—
their snow—is quilting soft drifts behind the spare
generator that the neighbor's snugged under cover,
waiting for emergency to glow corona-blue.

No, this poem's blowing to another blues-
storm: the wither-wind that aims to unhorse
a woman from her bones, to strip the cover
from her heart and set it out in icy weather.
She chills down to a slow stir, spared
no shelter in the soul's descent to snow.

If this were a poem about hope, the snow-
light would waltz beneath the moon, unblue
the haughty beauty of the stars. A spine-spare
trail would light her to the stable, to the horse
whose blown breath would warm her against weather,
whose deep heat would allow her to recover.

She studies the dark valley, hoping to discover
whether she can ride out the storm, unwind the snow
sheet from her heart, stiff in bitter weather
that ices her arteries from red down to blue.
She wills her thighs to feel an August horse
rising out of moonlight—saddle-blanket to spare—

who would bear her straight to heat, not spar-
ing hoof or lung, where the sun would draw a cover-
let of stars to warm her till she gallops like a horse
spring-loosed in pastures greening under snow,
alive to swallows pouring from the barn, blue
wings arrowed into heart-mount weather . . .

But she spares her heart the hope of summer weather.
Seals her bones, uncovered to despair. All blue-
veined, she saddles the chill horse. Heads deeper into snow.

BLUE HOOK

My blue-jean jacket's
got a strap
double-needle stitched

at the convex of the fifth
bone disk, and tacked
with satin zig-zag at both ends.

The strap's the means to say
who owns a thing
and to hang

the jacket from a hook.
When my jacket's hooked,
the strap

suspends the denim body
open on the wall.
Sleeves plead

to be filled. The collar
twists its neck.
Each seam exposes

warp and fray.
Cuff and yoke display
only dust, endure the careless

slam of doors.
My jacket cannot whimper.
Can't release the hold.

The strap confirms its stitches,
polishes and polishes
the hard blue hook.

BLUE ICE/BLUE FIST

1

She'd been warned to watch for blue
moon as though Mondays did not fall

hard enough across the empty bed,
the sheets blued in moonlight,

ghost trees falling leaf by limb, a splay
of bone-hand shading counterpane and pillow

across the quilt she'd stitched against all weathers—
hard frost, black midnight ice, raw red thumbs

of November, January's glitter-pain,
the sleet stinging kiss of March—

but not against the weather of his going,
the barometer's silver zero drop or

the stopped clock of mercury,
the slick dark harvest from her frozen garden.

2

Foul weather splits her window open
to blues the neighbor finger-wails at dawn,

the sax spelling in her spine, note by bone,
a shiver of elegies, a clutch of riffs invisible,

electric. Corona tweaks her blue
wire. The gas flame in the furnace fires

its butter-tongue, its tracery of red,
its brightest blue fist at core

unwrapping in blue flames
lapping in the belly of her range.

Their sigh—bright antidote to ice
and absence—can hiss her to kitchen,

spit a path to match. Can whisper
thirty years from England: *blue*

Sylvia fed me high and snuffed me, blue
Monday waits its ghost inside the flame.

The white ice of appliances attends her,
handles cocked to applaud

the exit of every weather—in a blue
twist, a white substitution for *exist*.

WAKE-ROBIN

common name for the trillium,
which blooms about the time
that robins return in spring

Shuttered in, behind the chill
   glass of winter, I
      am heart-shot

by April's pulled pin,
   her verdant explosions,
      glory-burst that shatters

rime to green,
   sleet cuff to leaf, ice
      to lace transparency.

Beyond my window,
   three copper beeches breech
      buds in raku shine,

foil to robin cocking sunup,
   breast and beak waked
      by trillium's cream trump.

Snow sheers to blossomdrift
   as Daphne's slow pink perfume
      seeps beneath my ice-stubbed door,

soaking parched mouth,
   March skin. The sky unseals
      for April—sunrise blushing

apricot, vermilion, plum—
   gift of Spring's milk-generous hand
      that next exacts the price

for pleasure: inches from my dazzled
    eye, she slams into the cracking sill
        her sharp-shinned hawk—

glass-stopped, talons fixed
    in one careless robin's redder breast.
        Hawk glares at me, and lifts the pierced

body. Wings to the dogwood
    where his stash wrings offerings
        into blossoms notched for sacrifice.

ARSON

Midnight—they are netted in flame.
Smoke nooses under every crack
and throttles them in place for the red
tongue to blister door and knob
and roar into the tinder of the top floor.

There is only one way to get out—
one apartment window, painted shut.
A smash, and her husband's blood
sizzles down the heat-peeled boards.
Fire races to embrace their bodies, the air.

He lowers his young wife by the hands—
four hands dancing in the scorch.
Then lets her go. She tumbles, ankles
shattering on the walk. Claws
up the landlord's hot chainlink fence.

There is no water yet.
At the window her husband glows,
swaddling the baby in his shirt. A billow.
He falls childless in the center of the flame.
Late, the rescue squad staggers in her voice.

Voiceless at the Sisters of Mercy, she sees
the other child flicker blue in the TV screen:
he shrugs his eleven-year-old's smile for the camera
and strokes the pet rat coiled at his white neck,
fingers still smudged with oil, ardent for the light.

CARD PARTY

—for Alex

Now pause, as mothers everywhere do pause,
one hand to curtain, knob, or nursery door,
to listen for the breath that lifts before
the silence of the heart stopped without cause.
Anyone may chide us: we turn and laugh.
Of course the baby's fine, we say, and sip
our wine, poke the fire, paint a redder lip,
refill the nut dish, play a heart, or pass.

And yet, the househeart beats elsewhere, above
the merriment, the card-bright air, the din.
We slip away to listen, certain of
a pillow slipped, a choking toy—our sin—
and, bent like tardy angels overhead,
we breathe again with him to heal our dread.

GALLOP

The day before she turns five, Amy hears
the doctors speak of her galloping heart.

The stethoscope has pressed its hard cold coin
into her chest. Air empties from the room.

When she is alone, she listens for the horse
that gallops in her ribs, for hoofbeats in her blood.

What she understands is this: tomorrow
they will sleep her and peel apart the fence

against which the red stallion beats tattoo
and let him out. Then her heart will canter,

walk an ordinary, one-two gait.
But she wonders—will he run into the sky

without her? Will his wild mane tangle in clouds,
and his hooves spark a starfall beyond the moon?

She sees an empty saddle on his back.
When they open the gate to let him out

(this must be the secret), she will hold on—
she will gallop too.

THE WHITE BOAT

There are the white lights lowered over the steel table,
then the white walls sliding past the cart,

the snows banked beyond the narrow window,
the white crumpled tissues balled in pale fists.

The paperwhite narcissus rooted in pebbles and water,
unfolding its fragrance as a salve.

The clear looped tube run with the milk
of juiced poppies, the ivory mirror turned to the wall.

The blanched fingers of relatives, snapping
open and shut, and shut, the clasp of a purse, a pen.

The august heads conferencing beyond
door 32B, lips pressed tight, bloodstopped.

The delicate limbs laid against white
sheets tugged tight to ward off failure,

and the small white bones rising to the surface
of flesh like the bellies of fish in a bucket.

*

There was Odysseus smashed free of his raft
on the wine-dark, white-capped sea;

and the white goddess, Leucothea, shifting
the veil from her ivory brow, from the coil

of her hair, from her neck like a swan's,
from the nook of her shoulder, white elbow, wrist.

Her white veil cast on the sea, her raft
wrapping him up and away from death.

*

There is the bright struggle against the white cells,
sails bellied and driving the blood tide.

The grape stain of bruises, seaweed rising
to float on the paperwhite skin.

There is the white veil of the sheet drawn
over the boy's body,

the body shining like a light
from the bed, from the bottom of the sea.

THIS IS THE TIME WE'RE GOING TO BE DYING

Verena Cady, 7, after the heart she shared
with her Siamese twin, Ruthie, failed.
—Summer 1991

As heart-wings miss a beat in their flying,
Verena sends the nurses to their knees:
Now's the time we're going to be dying.

Mother cups her mouth to stall the crying,
as two girls shed their body to catch the breeze
after heart-wings miss a beat in flying.

Their wrists blooming feather, they are trying
white egret wings on thermal rise and ease.
Now's the time we're going: to be dying.

Four hands release the knotted cloak, unguying
earth's ravelled clock. One double body frees.
Heart-wings miss a last beat in their flying.

Above the vacant bed, a blur is signing
their future—*alis volat propriis.*
Now's the time. We're going to be, dying.

We living watch below, unpinioned, pining
to catch—Verena did—the moment we,
as heart-wings miss a beat in their flying,
know the time we're going to be dying.

Alis volat propriis: She flies with her own wings (State motto of Oregon)

ABDUCTION

They build a bridge and send for you.
In sleep you cross, unbuttoning the house-
dress of flesh. Put on the crystal slipper.
Knot at your throat the white wedding cloak.

Then you marry cancer. We blush
to admit we would not choose to join you,
will not attend the bride in shadow lace.
You must embrace this distance and

the poison that defends you for a time.
You raise the alchemist's brass wedding cup—
we taste a bitter wine. As though we ought,
but fail, to save you—withhold

cure or sign. As though felons
have stolen you from home, delivering
a ransom note in foreign tongue:
we cannot read or speak it, and so fail to pay.

BREAST: STILL

after a photograph—
self-portrait by Matuschka

Her breasts sloped
under silk,

ripened as nectarines
ripen to brandy.

Now a ladder of sutures
brands the chest

she bares for the cool
eye of her lens.

We are invited to look
at the dark

spring of curl at her nape.
Rose arc of cheek.

Delicate
embroidery of bones.

She turns her gaze
out of the frame

that we may hold her
in our hands

and trace, unnoticed,
the new welt of seam.

Still, the deliberate
line of her jaw lifts

out of shadow. Still,
falling through the picture,

the ivory gown
chooses its curve—

framing the not-breast
so we may see it

for what it is: more
than the nebula

burst in the mammogram—
more than a gene's crooked stitch.

See, the artist says,
it's gone.

A sharp needle's mended loss
across her rib—still

she summons us to see
beyond absent beauty

to bloom of lip,
to pulse of nectar at her throat—

to all that speaks, and lives.

CARDIOVERSION

for my father

Because your heart flutters
    its leaves
as you would riff beneath your thumb
the pages of a book
    that slips at sunset from your grasp
    and stops in shade beneath the garden bench—

they pencil you in
    for emendation.

Doctors will read
from the ink-dark screen
    hung above the ribbon of your bed
a fluid green calligraphy
that diagrams the leap
    and falter of your truant signature—

the blood-pause
    that would bud its scarlet fist
and knot a black bouquet in your brain.

Surgeons will synchronize
the charged advance
    of plus-and-minus paddles to your chest.

Will summon to order
    your body's giddy scatter—
will override *accelerate* and *linger.*

Will attempt to reprove
    your fibrillating heart—

that white-paged butterfly
    beating and pausing

and pausing at the hinge of dusk
    to watch the last petal shut.

THE PHOTOGRAPHER'S FATHER

waits beneath this maple risen
    in its late liquid cling of sun:
        October torch, leaves flaming

out of their bones, slope of shadow
    layered down the limbs, burnish laid
        against the dark thrust of trunk.

Beyond, the llamas' pasture plays
    one last green reckless hand
        against the stop and snap of winter.

A low sun picks out pod and thistle,
    burns its last waxed threads of wick,
        candling for the camera

the maple's winged branches,
    turning leaves as they forget their sap,
        crooked joints where storm or swing

bent things out of shape. Deep
    beneath this brilliant canopy,
        washed almost wholly in the dark,

her father rests, thick arms propped
    across the split-rail fence, one boot heavy
        on the lowest rain-grayed rung.

His hair alone blooms
    incandescent, lit above
        the bodyknot of shadows,

shoulder's bunch, collapsing
    fist of years. One knobbed hand
        stretches past the fence, the dim barrier.

His fingers—his gaze—
      stroke the muzzle of a llama
            young enough still to know its name.

The shutter stops. Look,
      this picture: everything
            framed against the dark.

IMAGINING THEIR DEPARTURE

for my mother and father

They'll leave the lawn, hand clasping hand,
and walk away through sheets of light—
like light that sheers from pebbles and pier
beached at Half Moon Bay.

The sea will invite their skins with salt,
with white foam swash beneath the boards.
They'll kneel to unlace their canvas shoes,
and dangle bare feet above spindrift.

Imagine how he will take her hand,
and point to sails flirting across the horizon.
How she will shade sun-dazzled eyes,
lean close to his voice above surf.

They'll rise, bearing the shoes, and stroll
to the pier's outmost plank—his head
bending to hers as she speaks. Their eyes
glanced now ocean-blue.

And the afternoon light that tacks and reflects
from the billow of innocent shirts in the breeze,
from the float of their loosed, unraveling seams—
that light will begin to absorb them.

She will seem to blur in a shimmer of salt,
he'll mist all glitter and melt—
while bodies, transmitting light as crystal,
scintillate beyond body.

The sun will draw that luminous mesh,
a net of sea-mirrors, into the west
where waters deepen and twilight seeps in.
Where the sea unlocks its blue vault of stars.

PASSION

You are the apprentice: strap
blades to your feet. Try the ice.

At dawn, at two, at eight, strike
out from lake-edge, body prowed

into wind's scour. Unweight
the right blade. The left. Press

palm to brushburned cheek:
last night's snowy nick and skid—

twenty feet, brinked up
by shattered alder stump at shore.

Now crouch: read the scored
peel of shaved line

as though it were your palm's.
Tighten laces. Rise.

Set blades' compass north.
Shoot for the distant bank

where ice skims thin,
black water licks underfoot.

Some, they say, have shattered through,
drowned deep as night.

Remember,
there will be no moon. Strike

two matches: one
to hand, one to heart's tinder.

Begin. See how close
the blade can burn.